The Hebrew Alphabet

The Hebrew Alphabet

A MYSTICAL JOURNEY

by Edward Hoffman

Illustrations by Karen Silver

CHRONICLE BOOKS

SAN FRANCISCO

Library of Congress Cataloging-in-Publication Data available.

ISBN-10 0-8118-1883-7
ISBN-13 978-0-8118-1883-4

Printed in Singapore.

Text Design by Gretchen Scoble

Illustration Production by Michel Bohbot

10 9 8

Chronicle Books LLC
680 Second Street
San Francisco, California 94107

www.chroniclebooks.com

Acknowledgments

This book would scarcely have been possible without the valuable cooperation of many people. I wish to thank Alan Rapp for initially suggesting this project to his colleagues at Chronicle Books and steering it to editor Annie Barrows and her colleagues Karen Silver and Leslie Jonath. For their continued literary judgment and enthusiasm I am grateful.

Throughout this project, I have been indebted to Dr. Gerald Epstein, Dr. Lawrence Epstein, Harvey Gitlin, Bruce Halev, Neal Kaunfer, Paul Palnik, Dr. Steve Rosman, and Howard Schwartz for their helpful and varied discussions about material in this book.

On the home front, I wish to thank three individuals for their boundless encouragement. My children, Aaron and Jeremy, often insisting that I take a break, helped me to stay cheerful and balanced. My wife, Laurel, more than any other person, gave me the emotional support to complete this project and fulfill my own expectations for it.

Contents

PART I

The Wisdom of the Hebrew Alphabet

JUDAISM HAS ALWAYS REGARDED HEBREW AS A SACRED language, the medium of divine communication. For millennia, its sages and mystics have taught that the letters are no ordinary vehicle of expression. Indeed, the very word for letter in Hebrew—*Ot*—also means sign or wonder: that is, a heavenly revelation. It's therefore long been advised: the more we learn about the letters through both study and meditation, the greater becomes our inner development.

The Hebrew alphabet's origins lie shrouded in the mists of antiquity. Today scholars believe that a version known as North Semitic arose among northwest Palestine and Syria's inhabitants more than 3,500 years ago, and established permanently the phonetic sound, numerical value, and order of what initially became Early Hebrew. Already used in the time of King Solomon, this was the original script of the Bible.

When, led by Ezra the Scribe in approximately the 5th century B.C.E., the Jewish people returned from Babylonian Exile, the Square Script—a distinctive descendent from the Jewish Aramaic used in the Holy Land—became the preferred language. It was eventually adopted officially for the writing of Torah scrolls. Yet, Early Hebrew never entirely vanished, and was used by the second-century Jewish revolutionary Bar Kochba on his coins in defying Roman rule. Nevertheless, for nearly two thousand years, the Square Script has been basic to Judaism, and relied upon by our greatest sages for prayer, sacred study, and meditation.

The Hebrew language is comprised of twenty-two letters, five of which are known as *double* (or *mother*) letters, as they have two distinct forms: when beginning a word and when placed at its ending. These letters are *Kaf, Mem, Nun, Pei,* and *Tzadi.* According to mystical lore, they were originally known only to the righteous such as Abraham, and later, to Moses, Joshua, and the Seventy Elders of Israel under their leadership. They brought the knowledge of these special Hebrew letters to the Holy Land, where through the Prophets, the entire Jewish people came to use them.

It's also worthwhile to note that the Hebrew language originally contained no vowels, though the *Ayin* or *Aleph* were sometimes utilized for that purpose. Vowel signs were developed during the second half of the first millenium C.E., but they appear neither in the Torah Scroll nor in most religious documents.

In the legendary tradition known as the *Midrash,* Jewish veneration for the Hebrew letters was fervent. The *Holy Tongue* was the usual designation for Hebrew, which was even deemed the language of the angels. The early rabbis regarded the letters as existing independently in a transcendent realm, and taught that when Moses ascended Mount Sinai to receive the Torah, he saw God designing crowns for the individual letters.

Likewise, in Talmudic commentary on the Book of Exodus, the artisan Bezalel built the Tabernacle in the wilderness because he "knew how to combine the letters with which heaven and earth were created." The sages compared such mystical wisdom to God's in creating the cosmos, and correspondingly, included in the Talmud an introductory lesson on the import of every Hebrew letter. Similarly, the *Midrash* taught that King Solomon achieved great wisdom and power through a ring inscribed with a particular, Hebrew Name of God.

For the sages, the Jewish prayers are sacred precisely because their words are composed of Hebrew letters. In keeping with this view, they declared that persons who made it their regular practice to speak Hebrew would have a special place in the afterlife.

Dating back to Talmudic times, the Hebrew letters have not only been celebrated as holy, but also venerated as an actual tool for spiritual mastery. Traditionally, the two most preferred techniques have been *gematriyah* and *notarikon*. In *gematriyah*, words with dissimilar meanings but equal numerical values (since each Hebrew letter also has a number associated with it) are probed for their hidden linkages. In *notarikon*, words are broken down into sentences composed of initial letters. Thus, the first word of the Ten Commandments, ANoKhY ("I Am") alludes to the sentence *Ano Nafshoy Katovit Yahovit* ("I have written and given myself to you in this book").

From the earliest metaphysical text known as the *Sefer Yetzirah* ("Book of Formation"), Jewish mystics have extolled the Hebrew alphabet as the manifestation of celestial patterns of energy. In a section that has long entranced Kabbalistic adepts, this ancient treatise vividly declares, "Twenty-two foundation letters: He ordained them, He hewed them, He combined them, He weighed them, He interchanged them. And He created with them the whole creation and everything to be created in the future."

Based on this provocative notion, later Jewish visionaries stressed that mastery of the Hebrew alphabet—in all its varied aspects—allows the individual to gain supreme knowledge about the realm of matter. In particular, they regarded the Names of God as powerful devices in the hands of the knowledgeable. The correct permutation and pronunciation of certain Divine Names was believed to grant the ability to cure the dangerously ill, perceive events far away in time and space, and even to create a *golem* (a humanoid made from clay).

The thirteenth-century *Zohar* (Book of Splendor) is filled with references to the importance of the Hebrew alphabet as a celestial code or blueprint for the cosmos. Interestingly, modern science can supply an analogy to clarify this evocative concept: Just as we now regard the DNA molecule as a carrier of incredibly condensed information concerning the development of life, so too have Kabbalists viewed the Hebrew language of Scripture as a cipher describing the universe. The *Zohar* relates that, "God looked into [the letters] of the Torah and created the universe."

The *Zohar* affirms that every sentence, every phrase, every word, and even every letter of the Bible exists simultaneously on several levels of meaning. This sacred work clearly declares, "Woe unto those who see in the Law nothing but simple narratives and ordinary words! . . . Every word of the Law contains an elevated sense and a sublime mystery."

In keeping with this notion, the *Zohar* devotes an entire section to the subtleties reflected in the single word *Bereshith* (usually translated as simply, "In the Beginning"), which opens the Book of Genesis and the Bible.

Moreover, there is even a detailed discussion on the single letter *Beit,* which begins that first word. This approach to Scripture—and the Hebrew alphabet that communicates it—has remained central to the Kabbalah.

Abraham ben Samuel Abulafia (c. 1240–1292) was among the most important Jewish mystics, due to his development of a meditative system based on the Hebrew alphabet. Believing that each of us can attain lofty spiritual states, Abulafia taught in a practical way that the Hebrew letters are a key pathway—in fact, the means for "the soul to actualize its potential with much greater ease" than with any other method. He emphasized that through proper understanding and practice, any person can use the Hebrew language as a means to arouse tremendous, intuitive capabilities. "Look at these holy letters with truth and belief," he advised, "[it] will awaken the heart to thoughts of godly and prophetic images."

Abulafia taught that the path to higher awareness is not particularly difficult. He recommended that initiates keep themselves in vibrant physical health, for in his view, the human body is a sacred vessel. Indeed, Abulafia's yoga-like exercises, involving altered modes of breathing, require strong bodily vitality, or else actual harm might result.

The crucial aspect of Abulafia's system is the utilization of the Hebrew language as the vehicle by which we ascend into the transcendent world. He

poetically referred to this process as "knowing God through the method of the twenty-two letters of the Hebrew alphabet." Abulafia specifically advised his followers, "Cleanse your body, and choose a special place where none will hear you, and remain altogether by yourself in isolation. Sit in one place in a room, or in the attic . . . it is best to begin by night."

In Abulafia's approach, the individual "begins to combine letters, a few or many, reversing and rolling them around rapidly, until [one's] heart feels warm." Those who adhere diligently to this technique, Abulafia declared, will eventually experience "a plenitude of saintly spirit . . . wisdom, understanding, good counsel and knowledge. . . . The spirit of the Lord will rest upon [them]."

During Abulafia's colorful life, he inspired groups of followers throughout the Mediterranean region. To the present day, Abulafia's creative means for awakening intuition are practiced by people around the world.

In the ensuing centuries since Abulafia created his meditative system, many Jewish thinkers have extolled the spiritual power of the Hebrew alphabet. In the sixteenth century, Rabbi Isaac Luria taught that with the right inner focus—or *kavana*—the individual could use the letters for tremendous spiritual development. To this end, he developed complex methods of visualization involving the letters.

According to legend, during the High Holy Days, Rabbi Luria felt that his prayers were especially effective, but an angel revealed to him that another's prayers were even more potent. Quite intrigued, Rabbi Luria sought out and found the man, who seemed a most ordinary villager.

"What did you do on Rosh Hashonah?" the great rabbi asked.

Apologetically, the man replied that he was unlearned and could not even read the entire Hebrew alphabet. So, when the Rosh Hashonah services began at his synagogue, he had recited the first ten letters and said, "Please, O Master of the Universe, take my letters and form them into words that will please You." And he had repeated this phrase all day long. Upon hearing the simple man's account, Rabbi Luria then understood that the heartfelt prayers of the uneducated villager had been more exalted than all others.

The early Hasidic leaders likewise extolled the Hebrew letters as vessels of the divine. Hasidism's charismatic founder, Israel ben Eliezer—known as the *Baal Shem Tov* ("Master of the Good Name")—strongly emphasized this notion, both through colorful parables to unschooled folk and advanced Kabbalistic techniques to selected disciples. "Every physical thing contains these twenty-two letters," he commented, "with which the world and everything in it are revealed." On another occasion, the Baal Shem Tov remarked

that, "All things were created through combinations of the twenty-two Hebrew letters."

In Hasidism, the biblical craftsperson's name, Bezalel, means "in the shadow of God," for "to shadow" means "to emulate." Thus did Bezalel, through the knowledge of the power of the letters and their permutations, emulate God in the act of Creation.

However, as the Kabbalah began a long eclipse in the early 19th century, such ideas fell into disrepute. In the industrial age of the steam engine and the locomotive, Jewish mysticism seemed outdated. Its provocative ideas about the cosmos just didn't fit the prevailing scientific worldview. Outside of the Hasidim, few explored this vast tradition anymore.

But today, a growing interest in Kabbalah is truly underway. The reasons are probably many, and yet remain mysterious. Certainly, we now see science's inability to provide ultimate answers about the universe. Also, in the light of quantum physics, science and mysticism no longer seem so incompatible. Whatever the explanation, we're witnessing an era in which people from all faiths and backgrounds are rediscovering the Kabbalah's visionary power and wisdom. As part of this renaissance, the Hebrew alphabet is once again evoking fascination.

As Jewish mystics and sages have taught for millennia, the Hebrew alphabet bears a host of hidden significances. In traditional Jewish thought, each letter—its name, pictorial form, numerical equivalent, and respective position in the alphabet—is ordained by God. As a corollary of this principle, Jewish law has decreed for millennia that every letter of a Torah scroll must be perfect, or else the entire scroll is forbidden to be used. Not a fragment of a single letter may be omitted or distorted; nor may its individual character be compromised by contact with any other letters. Every word must be spelled correctly; one extra, transposed, or missing letter invalidates the whole scroll.

This religious dictum itself can be seen to impart a higher lesson: each person, like each letter in the Torah, has a unique purpose in the divine plan. No one may impinge on another's particular mission in life, just as no two letters may overlap.

The sixteenth-century Kabbalist Rabbi Isaac Horowitz declared that the Hebrew letters' spiritual essence was known to the angels and guided their holy actions. I can't promise that you'll inwardly climb to such dazzling heights. But as you contemplate the beautiful Hebrew letters in this book and the mystical lore surrounding them, I am sure that your soul will be wonderfully elevated.

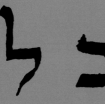

אלף ALEPH · בית BEIT · גימל GIMEL · דלד DALED · הא HEI · וו VOV

VOV	HEI	DALED	GIMEL	BEIT	ALEPH

LAMED	KAF	YUD	TET	CHET	ZAYIN

TZADI	PEI	AYIN	SAMECH	NUN	MEM

TAV	SHIN	REISH	KUF

Aleph

THE KABBALAH IS FILLED WITH REFERENCES TO MYSTERIOUS *Aleph*, the first Hebrew letter. It is the only letter that makes no sound of its own in a word—and yet from it arises the entire alphabet of sounds and infinite meanings. The sages regard *Aleph* as signifying that everything each of us accomplishes, however important in daily life, first emanates from stillness and silence.

In Kabbalistic lore, the *Aleph* is the outward, thrusting energy that seeds the cosmos. It is the primal force of Creation that exists before any form can even be visualized, for the Bible itself begins with the second letter, *Beit*, not the first. The *Zohar* teaches us that each person possesses some of this divine power, for the *Aleph's* shape resembles an individual ready to act in the world.

Aleph represents the number one, and begins the word for Divine Unity, *Echad.* The greater our spiritual awareness, the more intensely

we experience that everything in the universe is interconnected and composed of Divine Oneness.

For Jewish mystics, it is no accident that *Aleph* begins the first of God's holy names in the Bible—*Elohim*—as well as the traditional, esoteric name for God, known as the *Ein Sof* ("Infinite"), whose supernal vastness and strength lie beyond all comprehension. Yet, as the Hasidic leader Rabbi Schneur Zalman of Liady declared, every soul "naturally yearns to separate itself from the body in order to unite with its origin and source . . . the fountainhead of all life." For any Kabbalistic discussion of space, time, and human existence in the cosmos, the *Ein Sof* is the fundamental concept.

To bring greater energy into your everyday activities, meditate upon the *Aleph.* It is especially useful to do so when seeking that spark of creativity to forge a new project.

Beit

THE SECOND HEBREW LETTER HAS ALWAYS BEEN MYSTICALLY associated with a house *(bayit)*, for the sages teach that the cosmos, and our own existence within it, is designed to be a dwelling-place for the divine. In particular, Rabbi Isaac Luria emphasized that each of us—through our thoughts, speech, and deeds—helps to bring about this redemptive process. Consistent with this viewpoint venerating the importance of daily human life, the letter *Beit* begins the words for the holy Temple of Jerusalem *(Beit Hamikdosh)* and for places of study *(batei midrash)*, social gathering *(batei knesset)*, and prayer *(batei tefilah)*. Traditionally, we are also advised to seek peace within our own household *(shalom habayit)* as a spiritual ideal.

For Kabbalists, *Beit* represents the primal, receptive energy: the universal home, the infinite womb of fertility, from which everything is born and nourished.

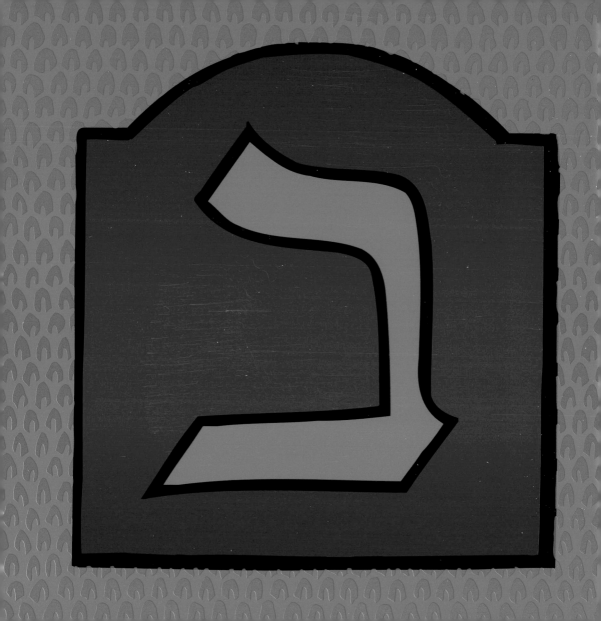

Relatedly, *Beit* begins the vital Hebrew word for blessing *(beracha)*, and signifies that our everyday life is filled with divine nurturance—if we are receptive to it. In Jewish tradition, we are encouraged to thankfully acknowledge the higher Source of our personal blessings as fully as possible.

Beit represents the number two, and duality. We constantly see around us seeming dichotomies like day and night, high and low, fullness and emptiness, spiritual and mundane. But all such polarities are ultimately illusory within the Light of the Eternal Unity. As the *Zohar* aptly explains, "The difference by means of which light is distinguishable from darkness is by degree only; both are one in kind, and there is no light without darkness and no darkness without light."

To feel a greater sense of blessedness, divine nurturance, and being at "home" in the world, meditate upon the letter *Beit.*

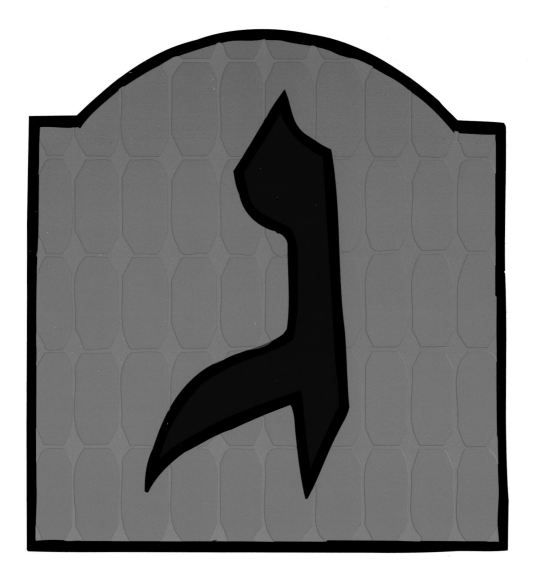

Gimel

"GIMEL" REFLECTS THE KEY QUALITIES OF BOTH KINDNESS AND growth. In traditional Jewish lore, it depicts a person running after one who is needy, in order to be of true help and service. Consistent with this notion, *Gimel* begins the Hebrew phrase for loving-kindness *(gamelet hasidim)*, signifying those actions of ours in daily living that benefit others. Each of us can exert tremendous impact in this realm—like biblical Abraham, who was revered especially for his deeds of kindness. As the Hasidic master known as the Gerer Rebbe declared, "Right work and diligence will bring out the hidden reward."

Gimel begins the Hebrew words for both exile *(galut)* and paradise *(gan eden)*, intimating that our daily actions unite these two seemingly different realms. In this regard, the Talmudic word *gamla* describes a bridge that connects two areas. *Gimel* teaches us that two apparently opposing forces must be blended to form a third, more complete and perfect entity.

Emanating from the Oneness of *Aleph* and the duality of *Beit,* there comes the synthesis known as *Gimel.*

Gimel also represents development, the process by which any initial spark of creativity must be properly guided until flowering into physical reality. Thus, it begins the Hebrew words for both great *(gadol)* and mighty *(gibor).* To accomplish this task when facing indifference or opposition from others often requires the key spiritual trait of courage *(gevurah)*— likewise represented by the third Hebrew letter.

Beginning the Kabbalistic word *gilgul*—associated with a cycle or wheel—*Gimel* represents the soul's repeating cycle of physical death and then rebirth on earth, in order to complete its holy mission.

To foster growth in any aspect of your life at present, focus on the letter *Gimel.*

Daled

THE FOURTH HEBREW LETTER IS "DALED," SIGNIFYING THE FOUR realms of the universe in all of its totality. According to the Kabbalah, these are respectively *Aziluth* (Emanation), involving the endless, undifferentiated energy of the divine; *Beriah* (Creation), encompassing ideas but lacking specific forms or structures; *Yetzirah* (Formation), containing the patterns or blueprints but not physicality itself; and finally, our own, familiar realm of *Assiyah* (Action), where tangible reality—that is, matter—exists.

In Jewish mysticism, everything that we see or touch—from the seat on which you're sitting, to the distant stars—must first pass through these three higher levels before manifesting in our own cosmos. Also, for Kabbalists, *Assiyah* is the realm where deeds—what we actually *do* in daily existence—are of key importance.

Daled begins the Hebrew words for doorway *(deled)* and knowledge *(daath)*. In the Hasidic view, there are countless gateways hidden around

us in everyday life. Each, like the seemingly ordinary bush that Moses beheld burning but not consumed on Mount Sinai, can evoke an encounter with the divine. Yet because of our own hustle-and-bustle, we often lack the spiritual awareness to notice these potentially God-filled moments and places.

Related to this notion, *Daled* conveys the frame of mind known as *devekut* (cleaving to God), a major form of Jewish meditation. Its core is an experience of intense melding or binding together with God. As the Hasidic leader Rabbi Schneur Zalman, founder of the Lubavitcher sect, advised, "The essential thing is to habituate one's mind and thought continuously so that everything one sees with one's eyes—the heavens and the earth and all that is therein—constitutes the outer garments of the Holy One."

To open spiritual doorways that are now hidden or closed in your life, meditate upon the letter *Daled.*

Hei

THE LETTER "HEI" IS FOUND TWICE IN THE SACRED NAME OF God known as the Tetragrammaton—*Yud-Hei-Vov-Hei*—and connotes divine revelation. Its sound, resembling a mere exhalation, teaches that attentive focusing upon the breath is a means for spiritual development. Many Jewish mystics, such as Abraham Abulafia, devised altered forms of breathing to achieve higher consciousness. The letter *Hei* represents God's effortless breath in forming *Adam Kadmon* (the primal human), and indeed, the entire cosmos.

Frequently in the Bible, when righteous figures like Abraham or Moses were addressed by God, they replied with the single word, *Heenayni*, meaning "Here I am" or "I am present." Why this succinct response? Because, the sages explain, we must be fully alive in the present moment to experience the divine. As the Hasidic master Rabbi Nachman of Bratslav declared, "Our world consists of nothing except the day and hour that we stand in now. Tomorrow is a completely different world."

The letter *Hei* itself suggests a means for attaining this lofty perspective, for it begins the Hebrew word for intensive soul-baring—*hitbodedut.* Rabbi Nachman explained this method: "The ideal time is at night. Seclude yourself and express yourself before God. Speak with all your heart about the day's events and search out the goodness of your soul. Do so to the point where your soul all but flies out of you. This is true prayer."

Representing the number five, *Hei* alludes to the five dimensions of the human soul: *nefesh* (physical instincts), *ruach* (emotions), *neshamah* (the mind), *chayah* (bridge to transcendent awareness), and *yechidah* (cosmic unity). Kabbalists recommend that we daily strive to strengthen our highest qualities through will and devotion.

To experience greater divine light—revelation—in your current life, meditate upon the letter *Hei.*

Vov

THE LETTER "Vov" CONNOTES SPACE, MASS, AND PHYSICAL WHOLENESS: that every complete, self-contained object contains six dimensions. These are: above and below, right and left, front and back. In this light, the *Zohar* interprets the verse of Genesis, "Six days did God make the heavens and the earth" with the explanation that, "Each day performed its action." That is, each day corresponds to a special divine force in the creative process.

The Hebrew word for confession (*viduy*) begins with *Vov*. In Jewish tradition, there is no vicarious atonement. Each of us is responsible for our own misdeeds and must redress them properly. Mystical legends suggest that it's never too late to mend one's ways, but as a result of habitual lapses and persistent wrongdoing, the power to do so can be taken from us.

The letter *Vov* is also the Hebrew prefix meaning "and"—that which joins together words, sentences, and concepts. *Vov* signifies that things seemingly separate and even contradictory—such as in a conflict—can be viewed as comprising a higher unity. With the right attentiveness, we can perceive the nature of that unity, and thereby resolve conflicts.

The straight, upright form of the *Vov* additionally suggests that only when a person expresses uniqueness can a meaningful joining with others occur. Otherwise, the effort at linkage is superficial, weak, and ultimately doomed to failure. As the Baal Shem Tov aptly advised, "Never seek to imitate the spiritual path of another. If you try to do so, not only will you fail in fulfilling your own path, but you will not do as well in the task meant for your neighbor."

To strengthen your sense of interconnection, and your actual social network in daily life, meditate upon the letter *Vov.*

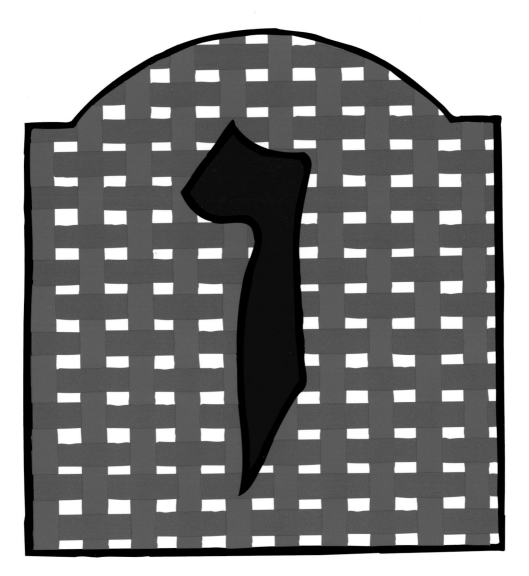

Zayin

THE SEVENTH HEBREW LETTER IS "ZAYIN." IT BEGINS THE WORD for time *(zman)*, which Jewish mystics regard as a key feature of human reality. In other universes, they explain, neither time nor space exists; but in our everyday life, we're all too familiar with the steady, irreversible passage of days. For, of course, time always flows onward and its presence is never-ending. Representing the seven days of the week including the Sabbath, *Zayin* teaches that time cannot be destroyed or even really nullified as a key force in human existence, but it can be sanctified.

Consistent with this outlook, *Zayin* begins the Hebrew words *zachaer* (to remember) and *zikaron* (remembrance). A people as ancient as the Jews might logically be expected to praise memory, but for Kabbalists, this trait has great spiritual as well as historical importance. For example, a key prayer during the High Holy Days asks of God, "Remember us in the Book of Life."

Hasidism teaches that to accomplish fully our unique mission on earth, we must recall vividly our essence as a transcendental soul cloaked in a physical body. But often, by allowing ourselves to become overly burdened by mundane matters, we lose our inner memory, and consequently, our sense of purpose. Thus, the Baal Shem Tov emphasized, "Forgetfulness is exile. Remembrance is redemption." On another occasion, he advised, "Whenever feeling downcast, each person should vitally remember, For my sake, the entire world was created."

The early Hasidic masters likewise taught that we typically move through normal, waking life in state of spiritual amnesia. So how do we wake up? One way is this: If lately you've been feeling rushed, harried, or impatient, meditate upon the letter *Zayin*.

Chet

"CHET" IS THE LETTER OF VIBRANT HEALTH AND VITALITY, FOR it begins the crucial Hebrew word *chai,* referring to life. According to Rabbi Isaac Luria, the letter *Chet* is formed by combining the two previous letters—*Vov* and *Zayin*—with a thin, bridge-shaped line between them. Thus, Jewish mysticism intriguingly teaches that our physical well-being—represented by *Chet*—is linked to the quality of our relations with other people *(Vov)* and our inner relationship with time *(Zayin).*

The eighth letter also begins the Hebrew word for dream *(chalom).* For millennia, Kabbalists have regarded dreams as a key medium for self-knowledge, inspiration, and even divine communication. The *Zohar* states that, "A dream is more precise than a vision and may even explain what is obscure in a vision." This sacred text also emphasizes that "When prophets were no more, their place was taken by the sages, who, in a sense, even excelled the prophets; and, in the absence of sages, things to come are revealed in dreams."

In keeping with this viewpoint, the eighteenth-century Rabbi Elijah, the *Gaon* (Great Scholar) of Vilna, advised his disciples that "God created sleep to this end only, that we should attain the insights that we cannot attain when our soul is joined to the body; for during sleep . . . the soul is out of the body and clothed in a supernal garment."

Kabbalists have long advised that we keep a daily journal to record our dreams, and that we freely share our dreams with those whom we trust. In this manner, we can enhance our well-being, deepen our bonds with others, and create a more harmonious society.

Chet begins too the Hebrew words for wisdom *(chochmah)*, and piety *(chasidut)*, affirming the link existing between these aspects of spirituality. In this regard, Jewish tradition has always encouraged that we unite our insights with ethical behavior in the everyday world. Ultimately, these two traits are deemed inseparable.

To experience greater vitality and physical health, meditate upon the letter *Chet.*

Tet

BEGINNING THE HEBREW WORD "TOV" (GOOD), THE LETTER
Tet first appears in the Bible with the verse: "And God saw all that He
had made and behold it was good." With its inwardly oriented shape,
Tet suggests that goodness is often hidden in our universe; as the *Zohar*
remarks, "good is concealed within it."

In Jewish mysticism, goodness is often associated with dazzling,
divine light. When Moses was born, legend has it that his mother,
Yocheved, beheld a brilliant glow and "saw that he was good." In similar
lore, the birth of Abraham was accompanied by a tremendous radiance.

Tet opens the Hebrew word for both purity and brilliance *(tihar)*,
intimating that our soul becomes more resplendent as we experience
inner clarity. In this way, each of us can emit a supernal glow to illumine
the path of others.

Tet begins the Hebrew word for travel *(tiyul)*, an activity valued by the
Hasidic founders for its spiritual potential. As Rabbi Nachman of Bratslav

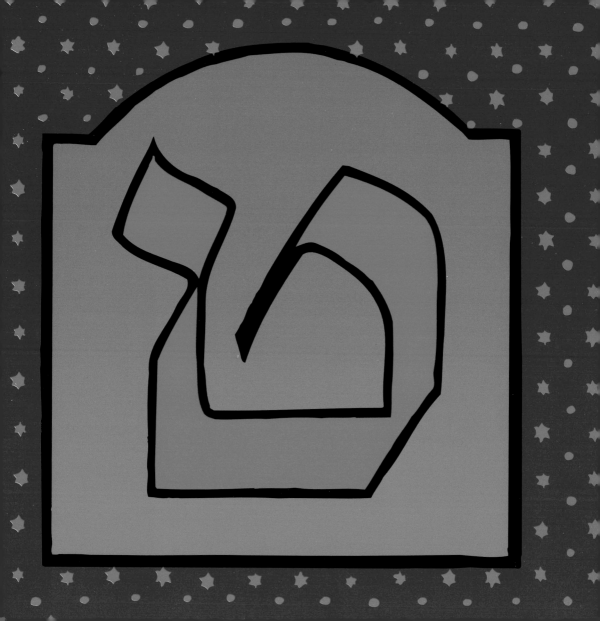

taught, "Each person is destined from on high to be in a particular place at a particular time . . . When you have occasion to travel, it is for your own good. If you would not make the journey voluntarily, you would be forced to go in chains."

Reflecting this mystical viewpoint about the power of travel, the philosopher Martin Buber evocatively stated, "Every journey has a secret destination of which the traveler is unaware." For in our new places, we may uplift the fallen sparks of the divine lodged in all things—and also see the world afresh. Perhaps for both reasons, many Hasidic masters advised spiritual seekers to initiate travel "and there you will find an answer to your question."

To strengthen your awareness of the true goodness (although perhaps concealed) in your life, focus upon the letter *Tet.*

Yud

The smallest letter of the alphabet, "Yud" is also the only one suspended in mid-air. In Jewish mysticism, it represents a cosmic messenger bringing movement and change into our lives. Traversing the entire universe in a micro-instant, *Yud* is the power of momentum too, by which an initially tiny dot of energy takes on greater and greater force.

Thus, *Yud* begins the Hebrew word for exodus *(yetziyah)*: that is, marching forth, rising up, or leading out. Likewise, it opens the Hebrew word for day *(yom)*, signifying that the seemingly small events of a single one of our days can exert incalculable effects upon the world.

In this regard, the names of many prophets and biblical leaders—human forces for spiritual change—start with the letter *Yud*. These include Israel *(Yisroel,* the name given to Jacob after wrestling with an angel), Joshua *(Yehoshua)*, Joel *(Yoel)*, Jonah *(Yoneh)*, Ezekiel *(Yehezkiel)*, Jeremiah *(Yirmiyahu)*, and Isaiah *(Yeshaya)*.

Opening the Hebrew word *yetzer* (impulse), *Yud* connotes our inborn tendencies for both selflessness *(yetzer hatov)* and egoism *(yetzer hara)*. According to the sages, the biblical commandment to love God "with all your heart" means "with both your impulses" —for both inner aspects can serve a higher purpose. In this sense, our *yetzer hatov* involves altruism, compassion, and kindness; and our *yetzer hara*, the passion or personal momentum that, as the Talmudists observed, leads us "to marry, build a house, beget children, or engage in business."

Representing the number ten, *Yud* is linked by Kabbalists to the ten forces comprising the cosmic Tree of Life. Together, these energy-essences, called *sefiroth*, sustain all of creation anew through constant motion.

To overcome stagnation and bring change into your life, meditate upon the letter *Yud.*

Kaf

First of the double letters, "Kaf" begins the crucial Hebrew word *kavana*, describing intentionality, willpower, and one-pointedness of mind. Related to the root-word meaning "to aim" *(kaven)*, this term has been a pillar of Jewish spirituality for millennia. For example, the eleventh-century sage Maimonides viewed *kavana* as essential for sacred experience and explained, "It connotes that one should empty one's mind of all thoughts and see oneself as if standing before the Divine Presence."

Rabbi Bachya Ibn Paquda, an influential ethical writer of the twelfth century, commented in his famous *Duties of the Heart:* "When one is employed in these duties in which both the heart and the limbs are involved—such as prayer—one should empty himself of all matter pertaining to this world or the next, and empty his heart of every distracting thought."

For many centuries, Kabbalists have prized *kavana* as the foundation for transcendental awareness. For this reason, though many types of

Jewish meditation exist—encompassing chants and melodies as well as visual forms such as the Hebrew alphabet—all are designed to strengthen and develop our *kavana*. As the *Zohar* declares, "It is necessary to concentrate heart and mind on the letters."

In Jewish mysticism, *Kaf* also begins the Hebrew word *keter* (crown), the highest of the ten divine energies comprising the Tree of Life. Kabbalists teach that the experience of *keter* is beyond all human speech and even comprehension; our soul on earth is cloaked in physical form, hence, we can catch only glimpses of the Eternal Splendor. As Rabbi Nachman of Bratslav poignantly stated, "You may have a vision, but even with yourself you cannot share it. Today you may be inspired and see a new light. But tomorrow, you will no longer be able to communicate it, even to yourself. I know—for the vision cannot be brought back."

To improve your willpower and intentionality, focus upon the letter *Kaf*.

Lamed

IN THE MEDIEVAL MYSTICAL TEXT KNOWN AS "THE LETTERS of Rabbi Akiva," the full spelling of the *Lamed* is read as comprising the phrase "a heart that understands knowledge." For the sages have long associated the tallest of the Hebrew letters—which literally means both "learning" and "teaching"—with true knowledge that comes from the heart.

In this light, the thirteenth-century Kabbalist Abraham Abulafia explained that such learning always has two dimensions: to initiate necessary action in the world, and to guide others meaningfully. That is, when our knowledge is heartfelt, and not merely cerebral, everything moves closer to divine redemption.

Lamed stands too for the number thirty. According to mystical tradition dating back to the Talmud, there are *Lamed-Vov*—thirty-six—hidden righteous saints on earth in every generation. In Yiddish associated with East European Jewry, they have been called the *Lamed-vovniks.* Released

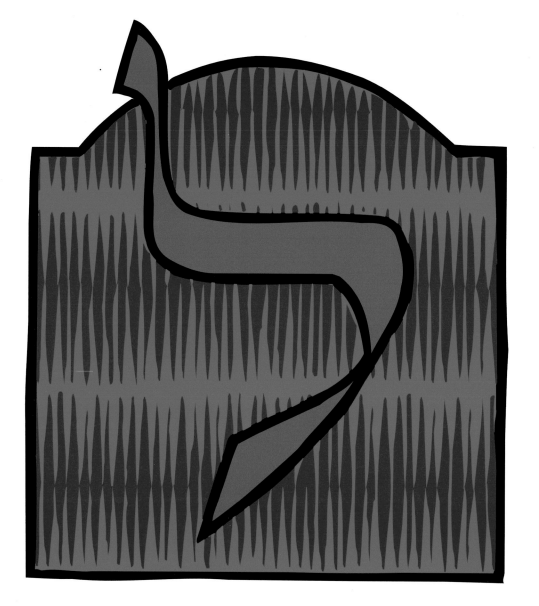

from the constraints that accompany fame, they quietly perform uplifting deeds—especially of kindness, compassion, and altruism—that sustain the world. In the evocative words of the Talmudic Rabbi Abaye, these exalted personages "daily receive the Divine Countenance."

Lamed also begins the Hebrew phrase for slander or badmouthing, *lashon hara* (literally, the evil tongue). Jewish tradition regards it as among the worst human faults, due to its divisiveness and destructiveness. As a traditional ethical text advises, "Be not like a fly seeking sore spots. Cover up your neighbor's flaws, and reveal them not to the world."

To achieve greater learning from the heart, meditate upon the *Lamed's* image. As the sages have affirmed, it stands as "a tower soaring in the air."

Also, think over the course of your life to date and ask yourself: "Who have I met embodying the *Lamed-Vovniks'* qualities of kindness, simplicity, and quiet serenity? And, how can I better express these traits starting today?"

Mem

As a double letter, "Mem" begins and closes the Hebrew word for water *(mayim),* and symbolizes for Jewish mystics the vast sea of human consciousness containing depths concealed from view. In the Kabbalistic outlook, we each have deep regions of intuitive knowledge and sensitivity seldom acknowledged—much less honored—in civilization today. Yet, these watery realms of spirit are vital to our overall well-being. As the *Zohar* poetically advises, "Just as the celestial stream flows on forever without ceasing, so must one see that his own river and spring shall not cease in the world."

Mem also begins the Hebrew word *maggid,* referring to both a wise teacher and a spirit guide. For in Jewish mysticism, when we attain a certain spiritual level, our mentors are no longer merely of flesh-and-blood, but can appear as transcendental beings. The sixteenth-century legalist and mystic Rabbi Joseph Karo experienced a *maggid* for many decades of his life as later did the Baal Shem Tov, who founded Hasidism.

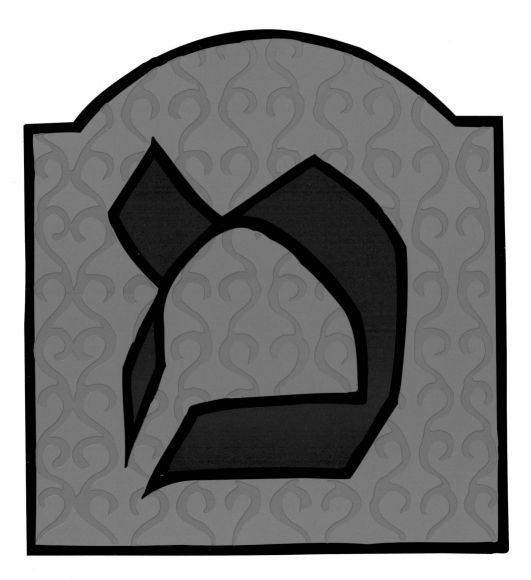

In this light, their predecessor Abraham Abulafia declared that those who meditate diligently on the Hebrew alphabet will gain access to a *maggid* as their personal teacher.

Mem opens the Hebrew word for angel *(moloch)*, literally meaning "messenger." In the Kabbalistic view, God often sends angels into our lives to perform a specific mission, but we remain unaware of their true identity. According to traditional lore, the Prophet Elijah become an angel after leaving earthly existence and, in disguise, helps those in desperate straits. Intriguingly, the Hasidic masters taught that sometimes, even unbeknownst to ourselves, we become divine messengers, imparting for others a crucial word or act to change their entire life.

Representing the number forty, *Mem* also signifies the length of time necessary for a cycle to reach fruition. For example, the Bible relates that the Great Flood brought rain for forty days and nights, and that the Israelites wandered in the wilderness for forty years.

To allow yourself more fully to experience spirit guides and angels, focus upon the letter *Mem*.

Nun

REPRESENTING THE NUMBER FIFTY, "NUN" SYMBOLIZES FAITH and its vibrancy in spiritual life. The Kabbalah teaches that while forty-nine lofty gates to wisdom exist in the world, above them all lies the fiftieth gate of faith. *Nun* is the Aramaic word for fish, denoting great fruitfulness, and indicates that faith brings us a sense of abundance in our daily life.

Nun begins the Hebrew words for prophecy *(navooah)* and prophet *(navi)*, signifying a spokesperson, or one who speaks for a divine power in human beings. According to Jewish mystics, this is a natural quality that we all can cultivate. As Rabbi Moses Luzzatto of eighteenth-century Italy explained in *The Way of God*, "One must realize that a prophet does not attain the highest level all at once. He must elevate himself, step by step, until he attains full prophecy. It therefore requires a course of apprenticeship, just as in the case of other disciplines and crafts, where one must advance step by step until he masters them thoroughly. Those

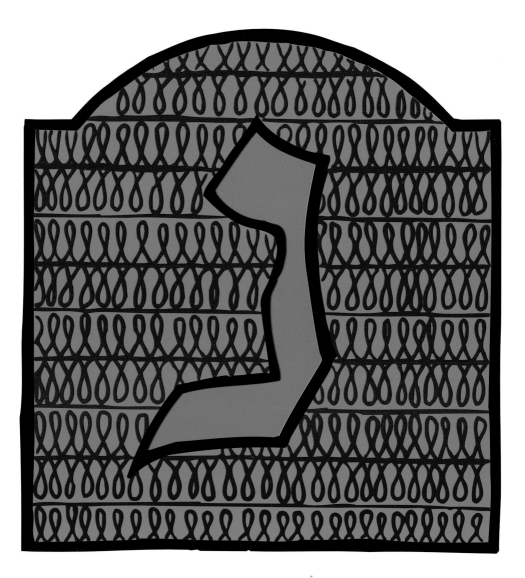

who train themselves for prophecy must do so through a number of specific disciplines. . . . In this manner, they attach themselves to God and bring upon themselves a revelation of His Light."

As a double letter, *Nun* opens and closes the Hebrew word *niggun,* meaning "melody" or "tune." In Jewish tradition, music has always been prized as a spiritual force, and as a doorway to transcendent experience. In early Hasidism, wordless music became a key means for helping people to achieve a heightened spiritual sensibility. In this regard, the Lubavitcher founder taught that a melody with words is limited and finite. The tune must end with the text's conclusion. But a song without words, he observed, can be repeated endlessly—and in that manner, raise us into heights of spiritual ecstasy. "Music has the power to elevate us to prophetic inspiration," commented another Hasidic leader. "With song, we can open the gates of heaven."

To strengthen your faith, meditate upon the letter *Nun.*

Samech

A CLOSED, ROUND LETTER, "SAMECH" SYMBOLIZES DIVINE SUPPORT
and protection: a higher power aids our mission on earth. No matter how
seemingly mundane our daily routine, Jewish mystics have taught, everything we experience is illumined by the *Samech's* radiant presence. For this
letter begins the key Kabbalistic term *Sefirah*—and its plural form *Sefiroth*—
the forms of divine energy permeating our entire universe.

Opening the Hebrew word for secret *(sod)*, *Samech* connotes the hidden
realms around us. According to our sages, human existence is a mystery
that ultimately only revelation, at certain times, can illumine. "At every
step we take, there are worlds upon worlds before us," the *Zohar* affirms.
Elsewhere, this intriguing text observes, "Whilst in this world, one
considers not and reflects not what he is standing on, and each day as
it passes he regards as though it has vanished into nothingness. . . . But
by word and by deed, we have to awaken secret powers."

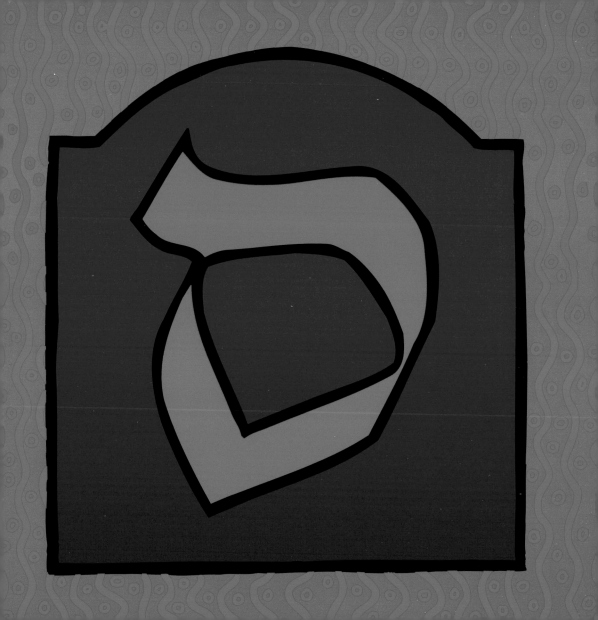

Samech also begins the Hebrew word for ladder *(soolam)*, a key symbol of inner journeying for Jewish mystics. It derives from biblical Jacob's powerful vision, in which he beheld angels going up and down a ladder based on earth and leading into paradise. Kabbalists have long interpreted this image to suggest that no matter how high our ultimate aspirations, everyday living provides the solid, crucial grounding for transcendent human experience.

In this context, the early Hasidim extolled the importance of stories—*sipurim* (whose Hebrew word starts with *Samech*)—to nourish our soul and give us a greater appreciation for the holiness existing around us. Such leaders as Rabbi Nachman of Bratslav cherished storytelling as a valuable means to wake people up from their inner slumber.

To strengthen your sense of divine support and involvement in your life, meditate upon the letter *Samech.*

Ayin

IN JEWISH MYSTICISM, "AYIN" SYMBOLIZES THE QUALITIES OF perception and insight. It begins the Hebrew word for eyes *(aynayim)*, traditionally associated with true discernment. The sages have long taught that as we grow spiritually, we gain greater awareness of the interconnectedness of all things and the hidden pattern of meaning underlying events in the everyday world. They have also emphasized that we typically move through our days with only limited sensitivity to the splendor that surrounds us. As the *Zohar* comments, "There are colors disclosed and undisclosed, but humanity neither knows nor reflects on these matters." Elsewhere, this sacred work affirms that "The wise person is one who, by the power of one's own contemplation, attains to the perception of profound mysteries which cannot be put into words."

Ayin starts the Hebrew word for tree *(aytz)*. In the Kabbalah, every form in the universe, including ourselves and one another, is regarded as a Tree of Life *(aytz chaim)* filled with the ineffable radiance of God.

The higher our consciousness, the better able we are to behold and experience this celestial energy. For the sages, the Torah itself is a Tree of Life, with beautiful branches reaching into all aspects of human existence.

Opening the Hebrew word for advice *(aytzah)*, *Ayin* also teaches that spiritual development always involves the help of others. For Kabbalists, we are hardly expected to grow by pulling ourselves up by our own bootstraps. Rather, peers and mentors are placed in our lives for practical guidance. Interestingly, when the early Hasidic leaders conducted spiritual counseling, they always concluded their sessions by offering specific direction for action. They believed that insight into a life-problem is valuable, but that it must lead to concrete steps for change—as Rabbi Nachman commented, "from the realm of possibility to that of actuality."

To increase your sense of discernment and insight in daily life, focus upon the letter *Ayin.*

Pei

MORE THAN ANY OTHER LETTER, "PEI" REPRESENTS THE POWER
of human speech, for it begins the Hebrew word for mouth *(peh)*. Visually,
Pei resembles a mouth with a tooth emerging from its upper jaw and
inverting into its cavity. In the Jewish mystical viewpoint, whenever people
speak, they release a spiritual energy into the universe—an energy setting
both visible and invisible events in motion.

As a double letter, *Pei* conveys twin messages. In its positive aspect,
Pei signifies that we ought strive to offer cheerful, supportive words to
one another. At the same time, *Pei* connotes the importance of silence:
of knowing when *not* to speak. As the Talmud advises, "To shame a
person in public is akin to murder."

Pei begins the Hebrew words for hole or opening *(poht)* and doorway
(ptach), symbolizing that our speech has the power to open doorways and
allow us entry into new realms of experience. We must never underestimate
the tremendous force inherent in human communication.

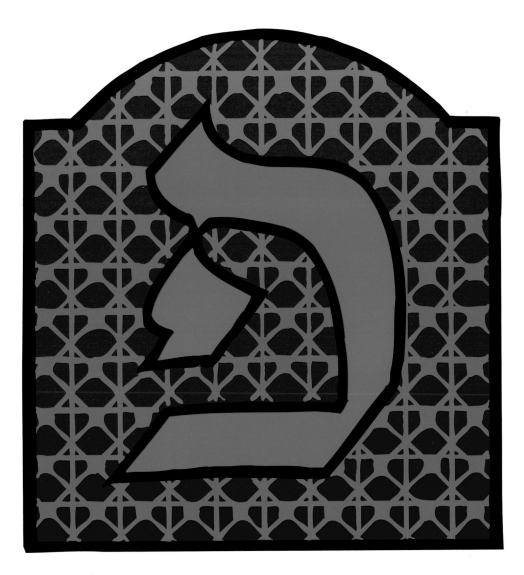

The title of the key Jewish text on daily conduct known as *Pirkey Avoth* (Ethics of the Fathers) starts with a *Pei*. Dating back to the third century C.E., this fundamental work is a collection of inspiring aphorisms for higher living. The greatest sages have recommended *Pirkey Avoth* as the starting place for inner transformation; Maimonides declared that to follow the discipline described in this text leads to prophecy.

Among its many suggestions for better communication, *Pirkey Avoth* contains this advice: "A wise person does not speak before one who is superior in wisdom, he does not break in upon the words of his fellow, he is not hasty to answer, he questions in accordance with the subject matter, and makes answer to the point, he speaks upon the first thing first and upon the last thing last, and regarding what he has not heard he says, 'I do not understand it,' and he admits the truth."

To enhance your ability to speak effectively—even inspirationally—to others in your daily life, meditate upon the letter *Pei.*

Tzadi

"TZADI" BEGINS THE HEBREW WORD FOR RIGHTEOUS ("TZADIK"), describing one who follows the precepts of Jewish ethics. For millennia, the sages have affirmed that *tzadikim* are those whose spirituality is never secluded or secreted, but rather, eagerly embraces friends, family, and community responsibilities. From this perspective, a *tzadik* is one who brings down the light of heaven into this rocky, mundane world, for as Rabbi Nachman of Bratslav taught, "One who is on the highest of levels can convey to you a true perception of the Holy One in all its radiance." Also, the bent shape of the letter *Tzadi* depicts our capacity to bend our will to the Higher Will, often acting through uncanny events and coincidence.

According to the great Kabbalist Rabbi Isaac Luria, God created the cosmos through a process known as *tzimtzum.* Beginning with the letter *Tzadi,* this Hebrew term refers to a withdrawl or contraction of the divine, so that a Void separate from God could exist. Out of that incomprehensible vacuum, matter and everything in the universe were able to come into being and develop. For our own life, this process has a parallel relevance, as sometimes we must reduce our inner forcefulness in order to allow others—such as loved ones—their own unique growth and learning.

Linked as it is to righteousness, the letter *Tzadi* also opens the Hebrew word for charity *(tzadakah)*. In Jewish tradition, we are encouraged to aid the poor and less fortunate not from philanthropic sentiment, but as a vital act of justice. Accordingly, Maimonides devoted ten chapters to this topic in his major treatise on Jewish law *(Mishnah Torah)*. His specific precepts include the following: Anyone who can afford it must give charity to the poor according to their needs; anyone who stays in a town for thirty days is obliged to contribute to public charity; and, charity ought to be given cheerfully, compassionately, and comfortingly. In his famous dictum, the highest form of charity is to give anonymously.

To amplify righteousness in your own life, focus upon the letter *Tzadi*.

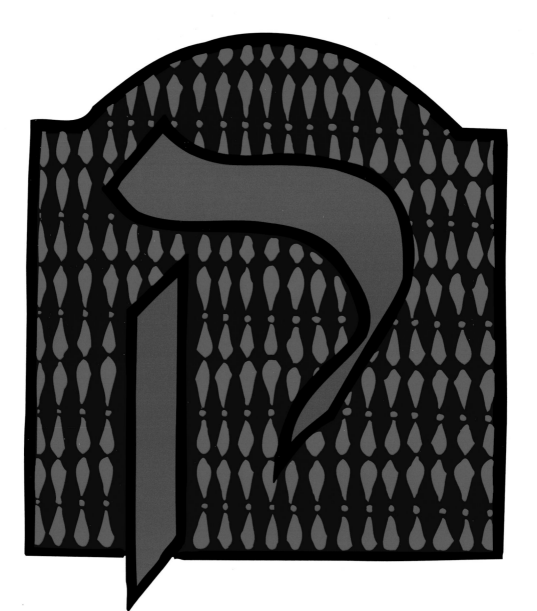

Kuf

COMPOSED INTRIGUINGLY OF THE LETTERS "ZAYIN" AND *Riesh, Kuf* begins the Hebrew word *kedushah,* referring to holiness and sanctification. In Jewish mysticism, we have countless opportunities in daily life to experience the Divine Presence. In this light, the *Zohar* affirms, "Whoever makes an effort to purify himself receives assistance from above."

Kuf also opens the Hebrew word *korban,* meaning "sacrifice," and originally referring to the burnt offerings brought to the Holy Temple of Jerusalem. For this reason, the Hasidic masters taught that to reach a higher spiritual state we must necessarily sacrifice aspects of our lower self, letting go of egoistic thoughts and desires, so that the holy can flow into us. Or, as Rabbi Nachman of Bratslav explained, "In seeking to sanctify God's Name, each person has something in his life which is more of a barrier for him than anything else. This is precisely the barrier he has to break in order to serve God."

Kuf begins the word *kabayl* (to receive), familiar to most Jews through its linguistic form in *kabalat shabbat* (welcoming/receiving the Sabbath), referring to the Friday evening service. Traditionally, we are encouraged to open our souls fully to the holiness it contains and can impart to our entire week. In broader terms, many techniques of Jewish spiritual practice, such as meditation, are designed precisely to help us attain a more welcoming, receptive consciousness toward the sacred. Indeed, for many centuries, the entire Jewish mystical tradition has been known as *Kabbalah* (that which has been received) with two specific connotations: that it is a body of knowledge received by humanity from the Holy One, and also by each generation from its living teachers.

To increase your spiritual receptivity—especially to the sacred flourishing in the midst of the seemingly mundane—focus upon the letter *Kuf.*

Reish

"REISH" IS ASSOCIATED WITH HIGHER CONSCIOUSNESS; IT BEGINS the Hebrew word for holy spirit *(ruach ha-kadosh)*. Throughout millennia, Jewish mystics have insisted that each of us is capable of great intuition, even prophetic capability, all depending upon our diligence and effort.

In medieval times, Maimonides taught that fear and especially anger hinder the development of *ruach ha-kadosh.* Much later, the eighteenth-century Italian mystic Rabbi Moses Luzzatto declared that "God ordained that one should naturally be able to teach himself, understand and reason with his intellect. . . . However, there exists another means of gaining knowledge that is much higher. This is what we call *ruach ha-kadosh. . . .* In this manner, one can gain knowledge that could not otherwise be gained through logic alone. This includes such things as information concerning future events and hidden secrets."

Reish begins the word *ruach,* meaning "wind" or "breath." Traditionally, Kabbalists have viewed breathing as a gateway to exalted states of awareness. Abraham Abulafia specifically taught techniques of altered breathing patterns, combined with yoga-like postures and guided meditations on the Hebrew alphabet. His followers down the centuries have recommended that we put aside time each day to achieve an inner calmness that can lead directly to lofty, ecstatic states of consciousness.

The Hebrew words for healing *(rafooah)* and healer *(rofeh)* start with *Reish*, intimating that our physical well-being is interwoven with the vitality of our breathing as well as our intuitive ability. In the Jewish tradition, the healer is never viewed as simply a fixer of physical aches and pains, but one who integrates mind, body, and spirit effectively. In the Kabbalistic view, all three aspects are interconnected.

If you wish to strengthen your intuitive sense—to better "see around corners" in daily life—meditate upon the letter *Reish.*

Shin

THE NEXT-TO-LAST LETTER OF THE ALPHABET IS "SHIN." IT BEGINS the word *shalom*, meaning peace—not simply as an absence of strife, but the presence of wholeness and prosperity. It also opens the word *Shabbat,* the Sabbath which demarks for us an experience of rest and sacred time, during which all is in harmony. For this reason, the sages have always associated the *Shin* with the rhythms of change in everyday life, ultimately leading to peaceful existence.

According to the *Zohar,* the letter *Shin*—which begins the Hebrew word for two *(shanaim)*—signifies too that for completion truly to occur, we must overcome dualities in our thinking. We are told that "The difference by means of which light is distinguished from darkness is by degree only; both are one in kind, as there is no light without darkness and no darkness without light."

The world as we know it is still moving toward wholeness. Thus, the thirteenth-century Kabbalistic text known as the *Sefer Ha-Temunah* ("Book

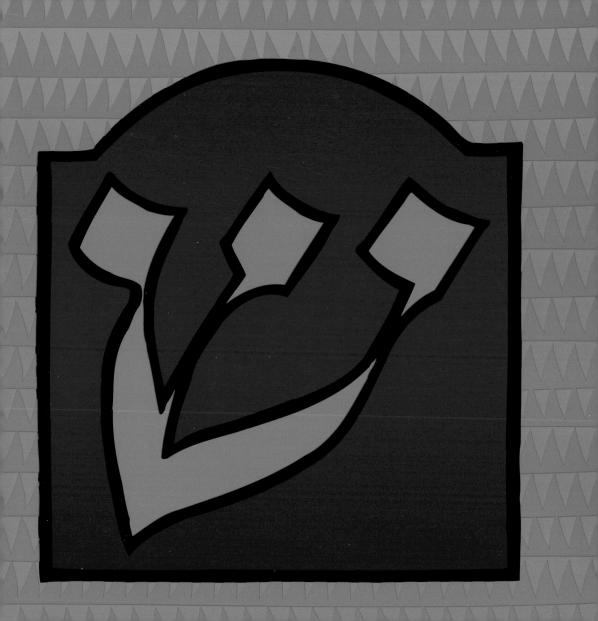

of the Image") intriguingly teaches that one letter is currently missing from the Hebrew alphabet. Every seeming defect that we see in the cosmos is mysteriously linked to this missing consonant, which will become manifest in the future. Some Jewish mystics have suggested that this unknown letter is a *Shin* with four prongs.

The Hebrew word for joy *(simcha)* begins with *Shin.* The early Hasidim extolled this inner quality as the essence of spirituality. Envisioning the "Great Sabbath"—the future Age of Redemption—as permeated with joy, they advised that we cultivate this trait now in everyday existence. As Rabbi Nachman of Bratslav declared, "Try to be as happy as you possibly can. Search for your good points in order to make yourself happy. The main source of strength within is joy."

To better experience a sense of peacefulness and harmony in your life, meditate upon the *Shin.* Since it begins the Hebrew word for year *(shanah),* it is worthwhile specifically to ask yourself: "How can I achieve greater wholeness this year?"

Tav

THE FINAL HEBREW LETTER IS "TAV," SYMBOLIZING THAT OUR universe is marked by cycles in all things—and that the ultimate end of this human cycle is joyful, complete redemption. It begins the word *tikun* (meaning "to rectify," "redeem," or "make whole"), a key concept for Kabbalists.

As Rabbi Isaac Luria taught, sparks of holiness are lodged in all things. In order for Creation to occur, shards of the divine fell into the world of matter, and it is the task of each person to redeem and liberate the sacred that lies within everything. For stones and plants, animals, ourselves, and one another, a heavenly exile exists until the Light returns unbroken to its Source. The early Hasidic masters emphasized that each person has a unique mission to play in this cosmic process. As Rabbi Levi Yitzchak remarked, "One must raise up these sparks, elevating them higher and higher."

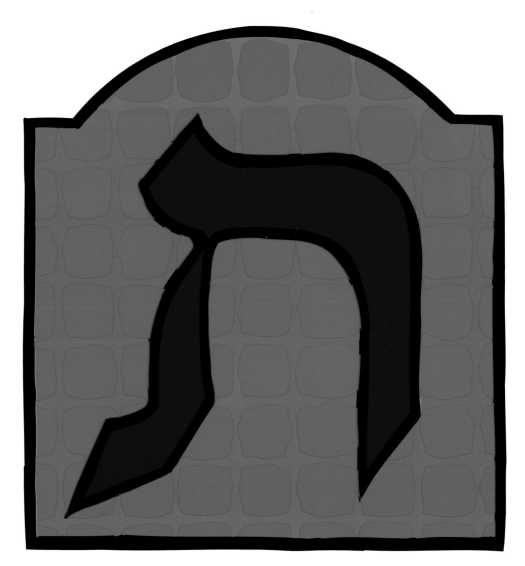

Tav begins the Hebrew word for prayer *(tefila)*, traditionally regarded as a natural outpouring of religious feeling and passion. Since Talmudic times, Jewish mystics have urged a fervent attitude when we pray; as Maimonides advised, "Prayer without devotion is not prayer. . . . Before engaging in prayer, bring yourself into a devotional frame of mind."

The Hasidic founders especially prized heartfelt prayer, and as Rabbi Nachman of Bratslav commented, "If you are not at peace with the world, your prayer will not be heard. Forget everybody and everything during your prayers; forget yourself and your need; forget the people of whom you have need."

The final letter *Tav* also opens the Hebrew word *teshuvah*, (meaning "repentance," or more accurately, "returning to the Source"). For Kabbalists, each of us is estranged from our divine essence to a certain degree; therefore, we must constantly seek to nurture and then express our highest qualities in the everyday world. It is precisely in this manner that redemption—and universal *tikun*—will occur.

To better actualize your unique mission in life, meditate upon the letter *Tav.*

Part III

Techniques for Spiritual Development

For millennia, Jewish sages have taught that the Hebrew alphabet is a valuable spiritual tool. Throughout the centuries, Kabbalists have emphasized that with diligent practice, we can harness the divine power within the letters to achieve greater vitality, life purpose, and meaning. No matter what our past background or present situation, regardless of time or place, this celestial force is always available to us. With the right *kavana* (intentionality), everyone can access the letters' energies for inner growth and development.

How can you accomplish this today? First, I recommend that you keep a journal to record your experiences. This is consistent with Jewish tradition, and will prove very helpful in documenting and encouraging your spiritual progress. I suggest too that you conduct the sessions at night, in a quiet room traditionally lit only by candles. The light should be bright enough so that you can see clearly.

Be sure that you will be undisturbed. Then, breathing gently through your nostrils for a few moments, feel a sense of calmness pervade your being. Be aware of the realm of holiness you are entering. As Abraham Abulafia advised his ardent disciples, "Take in hand pen and ink and a writing board, and this will be your witness that you have come to serve your God with joy and with gladness of heart."

Twenty to thirty minutes per session is quite adequate when you are starting out. Of course, you may wish gradually to increase the amount of time as you become more proficient with the letters. Through many sessions with groups and individuals, I have found that men and women typically develop associations to the letters that are remarkably consistent with age-old Jewish mystical writings. Many people also report quite spontaneous and uplifting spiritual experiences as a result of such meditations. These phenomena are convincing evidence that the Hebrew letters are indeed primal forces within our soul, just as the Kabbalists have insisted for many centuries. Who knows what else we will find confirmed within the visionary tradition? Let us begin to find out.

EXERCISE 1. *The Alphabet of Unity*

Get yourself a large sketch pad (at least 8 by 11 inches) or sheaf of white, unlined paper. A drawing pen with black ink will be helpful, though other writing utensils are also effective. You might wish to purchase a calligraphy set for this purpose. Carry out your usual preliminaries to quiet your mind; keep your journal close by.

Now, copy each of the letters of the Hebrew alphabet in order, as you see them on page 19 of this book. Take your time with each letter and do not skip any. As you draw the letters, each should have plenty of space around it.

During your copying, be aware that each letter is a symbol and a pictorial representation of a particular cosmic—and human—situation. For example, the first letter, *Aleph,* is characteristically seen as a glyph of an individual with arms outstretched in action. This letter also symbolically stands for the primordial generative energy of the universe. The second letter, *Beit,* has been viewed as a pictorial representation of a house, and a symbol of divine nurturance.

Let your imagination soar as you intuitively sense the statement that each letter makes to you. Remember Abraham Abulafia's poetic suggestion to concentrate "on all of them, in all their aspects, like a person who is told a parable, or a riddle, or a dream, or as one who ponders a book of wisdom in a subject so profound . . ." Note whether you feel a special affinity for any specific letters, for this relationship is significant, too.

You may copy the entire Hebrew alphabet two or three times in any one session. But after each sequence, pause for a few minutes to observe any images, thoughts, or feelings that may have arisen in your mind. These are not accidental or random, and at the end of the session, record in your journal what you have experienced. Whenever convenient, you may ponder their meaning for your present life.

EXERCISE 2. *Forces of Power*

Carry out your usual preliminaries; you will need the same materials as for the previous exercise. This time, select any four letters of the Hebrew alphabet that you find especially appealing and provocative. The number four has many mystical associations. Kabbalists, for example, have long preached that four separate but interrelated realms exist in the cosmos. These range from the radiant dimension of the *Ein Sof* (Infinite), beyond all space and time, down to our own, everyday world of matter.

Devote several minutes now to drawing the first of these letters in various ways. As long as the shape is recognizable, you may be as inventive, fanciful, or stylistic as you choose.

After you have filled your pages with many illustrations of the first letter you have selected, pause and be aware of any impressions that may have appeared in your mind. Record these reactions in your journal. Then continue in the same manner with the next three letters, likewise pausing after each one to note your personal responses.

As you perform this exercise, you will be intrigued to notice that certain letters exert particular effects on you. For example, one letter may induce a feeling of deep calmness, another may awaken the impulse for energetic activity, and still another may elicit feelings of love or friendship. Be aware of such results, for they are quite consistent with long-standing Jewish belief about the Hebrew alphabet.

You may also discover that some letters produce an immediate effect on your inner state, whereas others seem to exert little, or none at all. This situation, too, is worth noting. Those letters that you find most appealing are representative of soul-qualities that are vibrant within you. Letters that appear to

leave you cold are representative of inner faculties that are currently dormant.

Over a period of days or weeks, you may wish to focus specifically on each of the Hebrew letters. For just as all twenty-two letters are said to be harmoniously integrated as part of the divine plan of Creation, all of our internal aspects need to be balanced and arrayed appropriately. Ultimately, every Hebrew letter will spark for you a particular, heightened perception of the cosmos and its splendor.

EXERCISE 3. *Living Letters*

Perform your usual preliminaries. Once more, choose four letters of the Hebrew alphabet on which to focus your attention. These can be the same as for Exercise 2, or you may pick others. Concentrate on the first letter until it is clear and vivid in your mind's eye—that is, until you can see its lucid form even with your eyes closed. Jewish mystical lore relates that God gave the Torah to Moses as black fire superimposed on white fire; you may find this image helpful as you concentrate on each letter.

Now, feel your inner self soar upward and materialize in the Land of

Israel. It is the time of the glory of the Temple of Jerusalem. You stand on a plain bathed in golden and serene rays. You feel calm and filled with well-being.

Before you on the earth, vast and radiant with glowing energy, stands the same Hebrew letter. It now towers many stories high over the landscape; its apex rises far into the sky, its height is so great.

Explore the three-dimensional structure of the letter as fully as possible. Since you are transcendentally light and weightless, fly about, observing and feeling the letter's vibrant form. As you do so, feel the divine, living power that animates it. For, as the Jewish mystical tradition teaches, Creation is occurring at every moment and sustaining the universe and everything within it. Feel this power infusing you with creative strength.

When you have sufficiently explored the first letter you have chosen, let your inner self fly upward, return to your room, and merge with your normal being. After a pause, record in your journal whatever thoughts, feelings, or ideas you may have had. Continue in this manner with each of the other letters you have selected. As with the previous exercise, you may wish to perform this meditation with every letter of the alphabet, over a period of several weeks. This method will further strengthen the aspects within your soul to which the Hebrew letters correspond.

EXERCISE 4. *The Heavenly Shield*

According to legends since biblical times, Jewish holy figures have called upon God's guidance through a variety of means. Levi, one of Jacob's twelve sons, is said to have been given a divine shield by an angel in a dream. Upon awakening, Levi found the shield at his side and subsequently wielded it effectively in battle. Later historically, King David proclaimed in a psalm, "Thou, O Lord, are a shield about me, my glory and the lifter up of my heart." Many Kabbalistic legends have flourished about the use of wondrous shields inscribed in Hebrew with the Names of God.

For this final exercise, conduct your usual preliminaries. Now, select any Hebrew letter that you wish, perhaps one that already gives you a sense of well-being. Closing your eyes, visualize yourself surrounded on all sides by a dazzling golden shield—at least six feet high—pulsating with powerful energy. Imprinted and glowing on the radiant shield, in front of your body, is the letter you have chosen.

As you see the letter brightening in your mind's eye, feel its latent power protecting and invigorating you. It may be helpful to focus on a specific aspect of your life—such as health, livelihood, or personal relationships—in which greater divine support would be helpful. Or, you may simply allow the celestial energy of that letter to illumine your entire being with new vitality. In either case, feel the letter's pulsating power as it connects with your soul. If a little tune or song begins to well up inside you, let its harmonious melody fill your soul too.

After sufficient time, feel the radiant shield dissolving into the air. Open your eyes. Be aware of the higher protection and strength that you have just been given. If any thoughts, images, or feelings arose during this meditation, be sure to note them in your journal. Over a period of weeks or months, you may wish to perform this exercise with each of the twenty-two Hebrew letters in their beginning as well as ending forms.

Conclusion

The Hebrew language has inspired individuals for thousands of years. Its letters have been extolled as forces emanating from God, and therefore, deserving our closest attention. By devoting time and concentration to each letter, you will benefit greatly in everyday life. With regular practice involving any of these exercises, your soul is also likely to experience many new things. Meaningful coincidences, vivid dreams, or uncanny events may manifest, or you may simply feel more joyful and directed in your usual daily pattern.

Spiritual activity with the Hebrew letters is an unfolding process of growth and delight. As the Baal Shem Tov encouragingly wrote to his brother-in-law, Rabbi Gershon of Kitov, "Within each letter are worlds, and souls, and divinities." Let your voyage into those realms be filled with blessing.

Resources

A Mystical Journey through the Hebrew Alphabet, VHS Video. Written by Edward Hoffman, illustrated and produced by Harvey Gitlin. Commack, New York: Four Worlds Press, P. O. Box 695, Commack, NY 11725, 1990.

Ginsburgh, Yitzchak. *The Alef-Bet: Jewish Thought Revealed through the Hebrew Letters.* Northvale, New Jersey: Jason Aronson, 1991.

Hoffman, Edward (Editor). *Opening the Inner Gates: New Paths in Kabbalah and Psychology.* Boston: Shambhala, 1995.

Hoffman, Edward. *The Way of Splendor: Jewish Mysticism and Modern Psychology.* Northvale, New Jersey: Jason Aronson, 1989.

Kaplan, Aryeh. *Jewish Meditation.* New York: Schocken, 1985.

Kushner, Lawrence. *The Book of Letters, A Mystical Alef-Bait,* second edition. Woodstock, Vermont: Jewish Lights, 1990.

Luzzatto, Moses Chaim. *The Way of God.* Translated by Aryeh Kaplan. Jerusalem: Feldheim, 1978.

Schwartz, Howard. *Gabriel's Palace.* New York: Oxford University Press, 1993.

Zohar, volumes 1-5. Translated by Harry Sperling and Maurice Simon. London: Soncino Press, 1931-1934.

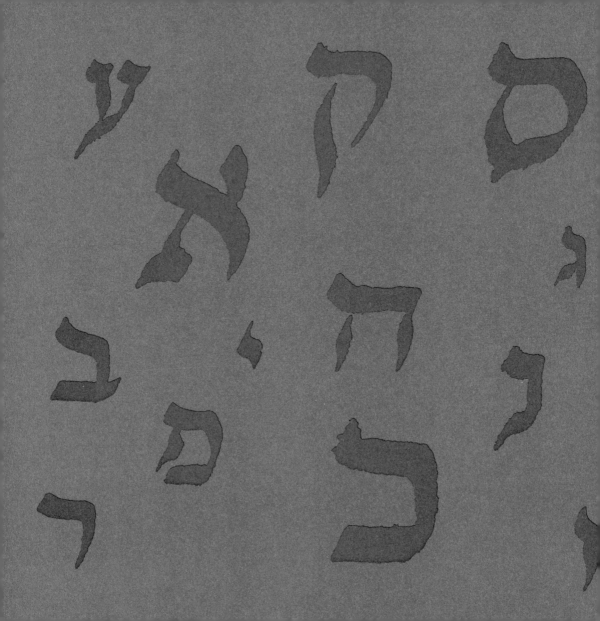